This book belongs
to

....

Once Upon A Christmas

TOM, like all the other children in the
world, sent Santa a letter with his Christmas
wants: roller skates and a paintbox.
But this year everything began to go wrong. First of
all Santa was held up by the customs. Then
his sleigh was given a parking ticket. And to
cap it all, Santa's ninth reindeer, the famous
red-nosed Rudolph, disappeared. Tom had forgotten
to write his address on his letter. Usually
Rudolph sorted out that kind of problem, but
tonight he was missing. Would Santa be
able to find Tom's chimney before
Christmas day dawned?

Once Upon A Christmas

David Oxtoby
Story by David Sandison

BARRON'S

Woodbury, New York · Toronto

Designed and produced by
Shuckburgh Reynolds Ltd
289 Westbourne Grove, London W11 2QA

Designer: David Fordham
Assistant designer: Carol McCleeve

First U.S. and Canadian edition published in 1986
by Barron's Educational Series, Inc. Barron's
Educational Series, Inc. has exclusive publication
rights in the English language in the U.S.A., its
territories and possessions, the Philippine Islands
and Canada.

All inquiries should be addressed to:
Barron's Educational Series, Inc.
113 Crossways Park Drive
Woodbury, New York 11797

International Standard Book No. 0-8120-5755-4

Printed in Spain

This book is dedicated to Tom, Yvonne and Nancy
Carlo Lorenzini
and Horsforth, as it used to be . . .

All paintings in this book are the property of
Ward 6, St Mary's Hospital,
Harrow Road, London

SNOW lay deep and crisp and even
(Just like in the song)
As Tom came trudging up the path
Which leads to Santa's home.
On tiptoe, he stretched out a hand
To drop his letter in:
"Dear Santa, I'd like roller skates
And a paintbox made of tin."

HIS mission over, Tom flew home
Quick as a flash, it seems.
For flashes happen double-quick
When they take place in dreams.
Was this a dream, then? I can't say,
For I could well be wrong;
But in the morning when Tom woke,
His Christmas note was gone!

NSIDE his house, old Santa slept
And dreamed dreams of his own,
Of holidays when work was through,
And islands in the sun.
His clock ticked on, the hands crept close
To when alarms would ring
To signal pandemonium,
And Christmas could begin!

CHAOS reigned behind the scenes
As Santa's elves got busy:
Such to-ing, fro-ing, up and down-ing
It'd make a top feel dizzy!
With cars to paint and dolls to pack,
And yo-yos put on strings,
And puzzles, games and wind-up toys,
And complicated things
Like names to check and lists to tick
To make sure all was right,
For Santa's journey round the world
Takes place in just one night.

HIS year the elves built something new
To speed up Santa's rounds:
A supersonic supersleigh
To beat the speed of sound.
They'd worked so hard to finish it
In time for Christmas Eve,
But though it sparkled and it shone,
The ground it would not leave.

EY ho!'' cried Santa. "Never mind!
Next year I'll fly by rocket.''
(He didn't tell them that he'd slipped
A spark-plug in his pocket.)

OR Santa likes things as they are
And not how they might be.
"Please fetch my old sleigh from the store,
And I'll use that,'' said he.
"We'll be some time,'' the elves replied,
"So while we get the sleigh
You'd better make a start on foot.
We'll catch up soon, OK?''

VERY few have ever caught
More than a fleeting sight
Of Santa Claus at work, because
He works so late at night.
And usually he flies so high
You'd need a telescope
To catch a glimpse of sleigh and deer —
They disappear like smoke.

THIS year, of course, was different
As he set out on his own,
And people were astonished
To see him in the town.
A group of carol singers
Were sure that they could see
A flash of red on rooftop —
But no . . . it couldn't be!

AND skaters on an icy pond
Were frozen in mid-slide.
Was it the Caped Crusader
Or Santa they espied?

BUT luckiest of all of these
Was a small boy with his sled,
Who had a perfect, hidden view
As Santa ploughed ahead
Across the park and out of sight,
His cold breath on the air.
The boy kept it a secret —
Now it's one that you can share!

HE news reached Santa that his sleigh
Was fixed and almost ready,
As he set out to row across
To the lighthouse keeper, Freddie.
"It's just as well," thought Santa
As he pulled against the storm.
"You can't land reindeer on a rock,
They could well come to harm!"

E left Fred's presents (woolly socks,
A fresh supply of candles,
A compass, books, new razor blades
And a shaving-mug with handles).
Then off he set, and made for land
Where his old team was waiting.
But first, he had to stand in line
At Customs — so frustrating!

THE man in charge looked most severe
And peered at Santa's pack.
"Have you got something to declare
Inside that heavy sack?"
"Oh yes," said Santa with a smile,
"Tomorrow's Christmas Day,
And if you hold me up too long
I can't get on my way!
And that means all the children
Who are waiting for these toys,
Will be gravely disappointed
And unhappy girls and boys!"
"We can't have that," the man replied.
"You'd best go right on through.
I've got two kiddies of my own,
And don't know what I'd do
If they woke up tomorrow
To find their stockings bare!
You'll want your reindeer, I suppose?
Turn left, first right — they're there!"

UT in the car park, Santa Claus
And deer were reunited.
I needn't tell you everyone
Was happy and delighted.
The reindeer grinned, and Santa grinned
As they set off together,
Across the crowded, frosty skies
As light as any feather.

OW anyone who's flown a sleigh
Can tell you, rooftop landings
Are tricky in these modern times,
And need quite careful handling.
But Santa is an expert
And his reindeer are the best,
So they hardly stir a snowflake
When they first come down to rest.

MAYBE you've stopped to wonder
About Santa and his sack,
And how he gets down chimneys
With that load upon his back.
The answer is — it's magic
Once more coming into play,
And he moves like pure greased lightning
Once he's really on his way!

THERE is a well-known saying
About the plans of mice and men,
And how things seem to be just right
But all go wrong again.
That's how it was for Santa
As he recommenced his round,
For as he clambered from a stack,
This is what he found . . .

"OU can't give me a parking ticket!"
Santa told the warden.
"I always park on this roof here!"
"Oh dear, I beg your pardon!"
The warden said sarcastically
As she surveyed the reindeer.
"I'm booking you — these eight hippos too —
You're in a no-sleigh area!"

"TUFF and nonsense!" Santa said.
"And anyway, there's nine.
And they're not hippos, or giraffes —
They're reindeer, and they're mine!"

"HERE'S only eight," the warden sniffed,
"But that is academic.
If we let you land rhinos here,
It could start an epidemic!"
With that she went, in dudgeon high,
Leaving Santa feeling troubled,
For there *were* only eight deer left,
And so his troubles doubled.

FOR when he counted them again
To double-check for error,
The missing deer was Rudolph
(The famous red-nosed fella).
And Rudolph is the one who knows
Where every present's bound.
He knows directions and locations,
Each single inch of ground.

THE other reindeer couldn't help
They only knew he'd gone,
(Though where and why they couldn't tell,
And neither for how long).
"A pretty pickle!" Santa thought,
While trying not to flap.
"Since I can't use young Rudolph's nose
I'll have to work by map!"

Merry Christmas *and a Happy New Year* Ward 6.

E'LL turn up soon, I have no doubt,
To lead us on our way.
It will affect my schedule, though,
And cause us some delay!''
He hopped on to a passing cloud
And peered around in vain.
For Rudolph had completely gone —
That much was clearly plain.

HE next few calls were simple
Much to Santa Claus' delight,
And then he made for Halfway House
(It was halfway through the night).
There, fresh supplies were waiting
To be loaded on the sleigh,
And Santa asked if Rudolph
Had been seen along this way.

HE elves were just as puzzled,
And were just as much perplexed,
But none could make suggestions
As to what he should do next.
They had another problem, too,
Which caused him fresh alarm,
For they had presents packed to go
With no addresses on!

 HEY say 'To Tom'," the elves declared,
"But that's our only clue.
We've searched our files and scratched our
          heads,
But can't think what to do!"

 H, botheration!" Santa cried.
"What more can go amiss!"
Jet propulsion, parking tickets,
Then Rudolph goes, now this!"
He left the stores with his new load,
And stopped along the way
To ask the North Wind Giant: "Could
You hold your breath till day?"
The Giant smiled; he understood,
And promised not to blow.
"But you'll get a gust from time to time —
I have to breathe, you know!"

 E also said that he would keep
An eye out through the night,
In case a wandering Rudolph
Should come trotting into sight.

M EANWHILE . . .

E VERYONE was sleeping, snug
As bugs in young Tom's house,
Except for Puddin, his small cat,
And his even smaller mouse
(Whose name was Arthur, by the way,
And Arthur was quite worried).
"He's never been this late before,"
He said, then quickly scurried
Across the garden, deep with snow,
To get a better view.
But though he looked, and peered, and stared,
He spotted nothing new.
No Santa Claus in coat of red,
No reindeer and no sleigh,
But worst of all, no presents for
Young Tom on Christmas Day!

BUT I can tell you, Santa Claus
Has never given up.
With gifts delivered (thanks to map),
He sent his reindeer off:
"You find that rascal Rudolph,
And you tell him to go home.
I'm sure in time I'll find this Tom,
But I'll do it on my own."

 snowman who had overheard,
Said: "Do my ears deceive?
I know a boy called Thomas.
He built me, I do believe!
He also gave me this old scarf,
And these old gloves and hat."
But Santa checked his list and sighed,
"Wrong Tom," he said. "Alas!"

SANTA carried on his way,
When suddenly — a noise
Of trumpets, fiddles and trombones,
And laughing girls and boys!
He peered in great astonishment
At what he saw within,
It was, of course, a pantomime,
The source of all this din.

BUT though he asked the manager,
The actors and the crew,
It seemed that no one could assist,
And so his problem grew.
His spirits sagged, his big sack dragged,
His hopes were so forlorn.
There seemed no way that he could find
Young Tom before the dawn!

IGHTS from an artist's studio
Caught Santa's eyes just then.
Inside, he found a painter
Hard at work with brush and pen.
Amid a pile of paints and pots,
And other tools of trade,
A wonderful new masterpiece
Was slowly being made.

HE artist listened carefully
To Santa's tale of woe,
Then said: "I know — I've got it!
Why don't I, before you go,
Draw up a picture of this boy
To help you win this race?"
But Santa sighed, "No good!" he cried.
"I've never seen his face."

WHILE seeking inspiration
(And a place to warm his feet!)
Old Santa sipped a cup of tea
And had a bite to eat.
He asked around if anyone
Could help him in his quest:
"One clue is all I need," he said,
"And I can do the rest."

A man at the next table said
He knew someone called Tom.
But he was eighty-five years old,
So couldn't be the one.
With heavy heart (but warmer feet)
Santa went on his way,
But had a mix-up with his hat,
Which caused him more delay!

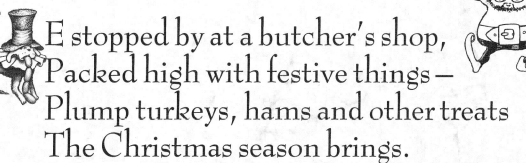

E stopped by at a butcher's shop,
Packed high with festive things—
Plump turkeys, hams and other treats
The Christmas season brings.

HE butcher listened to his tale,
But smiled a rueful smile:
"I'd help you if I could," he said.
"Why don't you rest awhile?"

I must get on!" the old man cried.
"But thank you, all the same.
For I have my reputation
To consider—and my name."

 rose for Christmas, dear kind sir?"
A voice called in the street,
And Santa saw a flower seller
Tired, and cold, and weak.

E bought a rose, then searched his sack
To find a gift for her.
He found a bonnet for her head
And slippers lined with fur.

HE woman thanked him for his thought.
"You're welcome," Santa said.
"It's far too cold for one so old,
You should be home in bed."

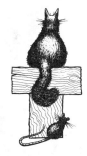

HE hours flew by so quickly
And daylight crept so near.
Then Santa met a watchman
Who helped lift his dark despair.
"I know most folk around these parts,"
He said. "So you tell me
What's in those boxes for this boy —
They'll give a clue, maybe."

OOD thinking, watchman!" Santa cried.
"I never thought of that.
Let's see — a paintbox, skates . . . and, yes,
Things for a mouse and cat!"
"A cat and mouse?" the watchman asked.
"Then there is only one
Who answers that description.
You want Tom, the farmer's son!"

E'S quite a lad," the watchman said,
"And loves to paint and draw.
I know he's set his heart upon
A pair of skates, for sure.
He also has a little cat
Called Puddin — and a mouse.
I'm certain he's the Tom you want,
I'll help you find his house."

HE directions he gave Santa
Were as clear as clear can be.
But even with them, Santa
Went off-course a mile or three.
As dawn crept close, the old man knew
He'd taken the wrong lane,
But he met a local shepherd
Who set him right again.

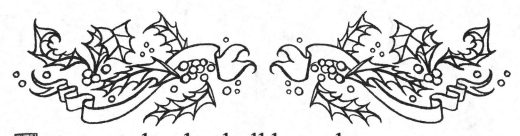

WHILE this had all been happening,
Tom's mouse and cat gave up.
"I think it's safe for us to say
Our master's out of luck,"
Said Arthur, in a tearful voice
To his larger, furry chum.
But Puddin made no answer,
She just sat there, looking glum.

FAR out there, in the whiteness,
She thought she saw some red —
A glimpse at first, no more than that,
But then she turned her head:
"He's made it, Arthur! Come and look!
He's heading up the drive,
With beard and sack, and big black boots.
Look — Santa has arrived!"

 OU never saw such howdy-dos
As when Santa clambered in.
For Puddin purred, miaowed and stretched
And Arthur did a spin.
"We thought you had forgotten us!"
He squeaked, his face alight.
Then his eyes (and Puddin's) widened
As they heard of Santa's plight.

 O Rudolph?" queried Puddin.
"And no address at all?
Then you have our admiration
For managing this call!
Most people would have given up,
A long, long time ago!"
"I almost did, a time or two!"
Santa whispered to them, low.

HERE still remained the mystery
Of Rudolph's disappearance.
"I hope this won't turn out to be
An annual occurrence,"
The old man thought, as home he walked
Through Christmas dawn so bright.
But then he was astonished by
An unexpected sight.

have a troupe of elephants,"
The circus man replied
When Santa asked politely
If young Rudolph he had spied.
"But I regret to tell you
That I haven't any deer,
Though I wish you Merry Christmas,
And a prosperous New Year!"

 N the morning after Christmas,
Santa snoozed before the fire,
Filled with turkey and plum pudding,
And a firmly-held desire
To spend the rest of winter
In this lazy kind of way,
When all at once he heard the sound
Of bells from far away!

 HE sound grew closer, closer still,
Until it stopped quite near.
The muffled sound of hooves on snow,
And then a face appeared.
At last, young Rudolph had returned,
His travels to recall.
But that's another story, so for now
Goodbye — that's all!